EARLY YEARS IN INDIA

WOBINE ISHWARAN

Author's Tranquility Press
MARIETTA, GEORGIA

Wobine Ishwaran/Author's Tranquility Press
2706 Station Club Drive SW
Marietta, GA 30060
www.authorstranquilitypress.com

Ordering Information:
Quantity sales. Special discounts are available on quantity purchases by corporations, associations, and others. For details, contact the "Special Sales Department" at the address above.

Early Years in India/Wobine Ishwaran
Hardback: 978-1-959453-22-2
Paperback: 978-1-959453-23-9
eBook: 978-1-959453-24-6

Contents

To my daughter Arundhati

And special mention to the Guru's:

The late Shivakumara Swamiji

And the reigning Dr. Shivamurthy Swamiji of the Sirigere

Matt, who both guided our Destiny

Acknowledgments

India became my second home, with its culture
colourful elegant clothing and its friendly people.
I was very happy living with my husband, my children and
his family members, at the Karnatak University Campus in
Dharwar.

My thanks go to my daughter Arundhati who copy edited my
writing so carefully and encouraging me to keep at it.
My children, their families and grandchildren who always
supported me, and my niece Smita who put together the Indian
family tree.

PROLOGUE

Growing up in an Indian village.

Chennappa Gouda was standing in his newly planted wheat fields, surveying the landscape.

The rains had come on time and the new crops showing the first green tips with the promise of a rich harvest.

The evening sunset glowing with radiant colours brought Chennappa a feeling of satisfaction with his day.

A melodious sound of songs, sung by the people homeward bond after the day's hard work on the fields vibrated through the hills around the village.

Chennappa was thinking about his oldest son, Ishwaran,

who came home to say goodbye to the friends and family of his village, Hiremallur.

In a few days he would leave the country to continue his studies in Oxford England. Chennappa was sad to see him go, and maybe never return, but he was a very proud father too!

It was very hard on Basawa, his wife and mother of the boy, she too thought, that goodbye, might be forever!

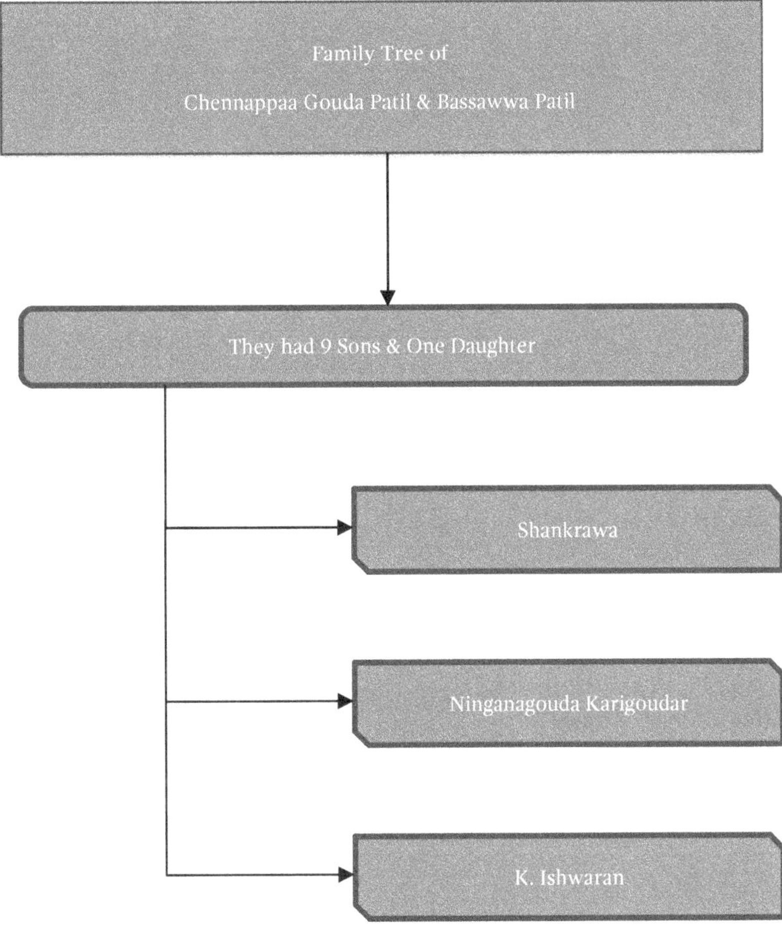

Family Tree of
Chennappaa Gouda Patil & Bassawwa Patil
They had 9 Sons & One Daughter
Shankrawa
Ninganagouda Karigoudar
K. Ishwaran

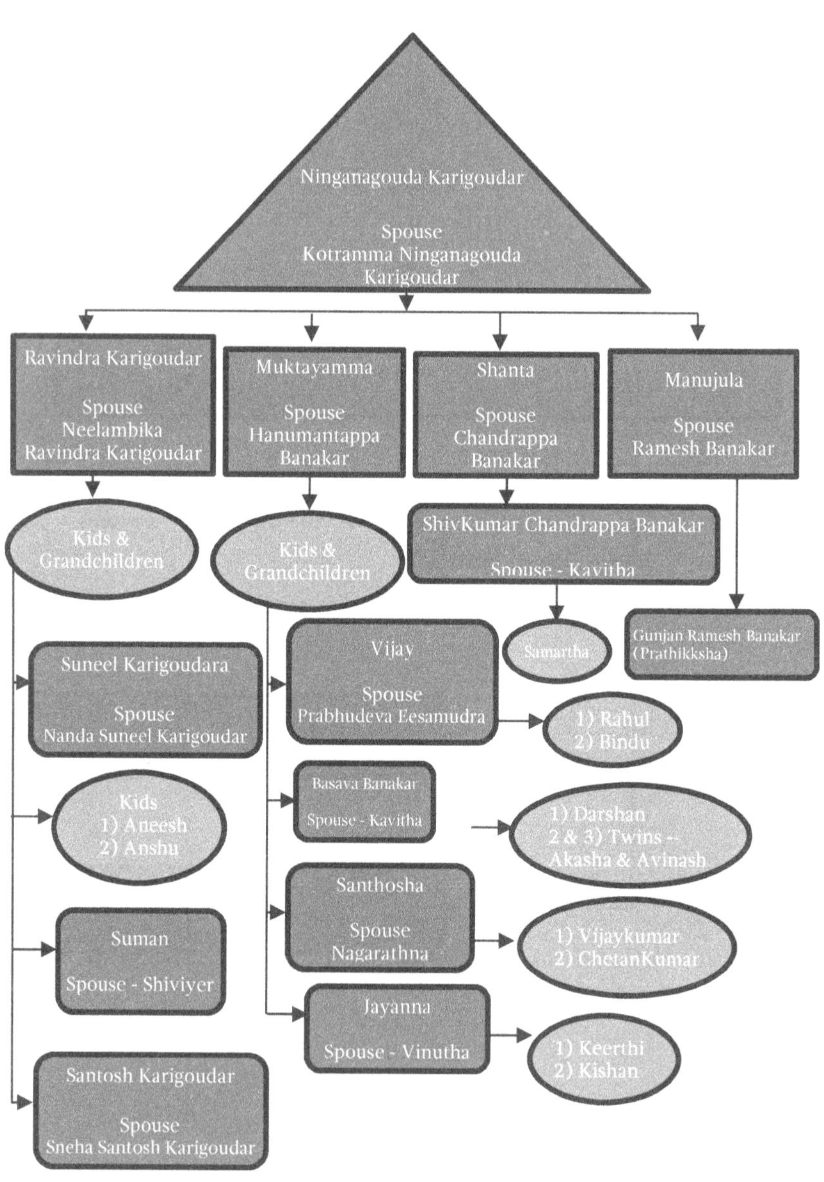

Ninganagouda Karigoudar
Spouse
Kotramma Ninganagouda Karigoudar

Ravindra Karigoudar
Spouse
Neelambika Ravindra Karigoudar

Muktayamma
Spouse
Hanumantappa Banakar

Shanta
Spouse
Chandrappa Banakar

Manujula
Spouse
Ramesh Banakar

Kids & Grandchildren

Kids & Grandchildren

ShivKumar Chandrappa Banakar
Spouse - Kavitha

Samartha

Gunjan Ramesh Banakar (Prathikksha)

Suneel Karigoudara
Spouse
Nanda Suneel Karigoudar

Vijay
Spouse
Prabhudeva Eesamudra

1) Rahul
2) Bindu

Kids
1) Aneesh
2) Anshu

Basava Banakar
Spouse - Kavitha

1) Darshan
2 & 3) Twins -- Akasha & Avinash

Suman
Spouse - Shiviyer

Santhosha
Spouse
Nagarathna

1) Vijaykumar
2) ChetanKumar

Jayanna
Spouse - Vinutha

1) Keerthi
2) Kishan

Santosh Karigoudar
Spouse
Sneha Santosh Karigoudar

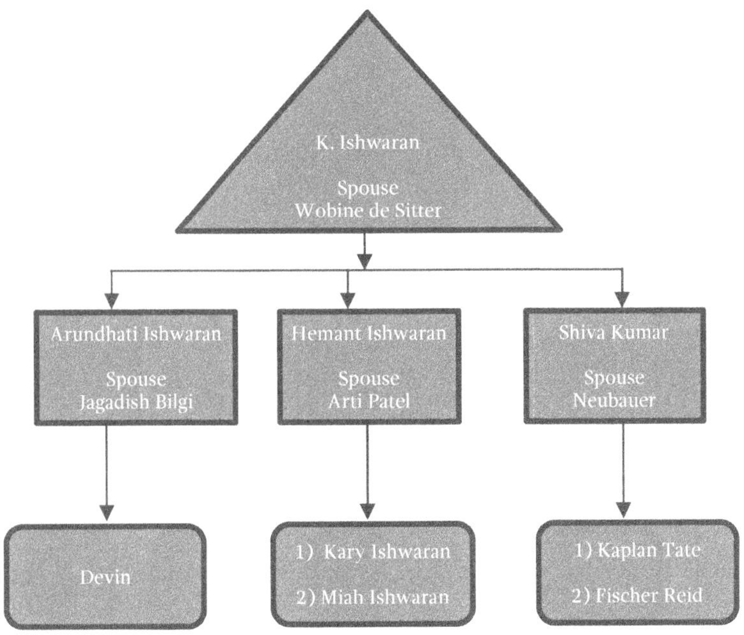

K. Ishwaran
Spouse
Wobine de Sitter
Arundhati Ishwaran
Spouse
Jagadish Bilgi
Hemant Ishwaran
Spouse
Arti Patel
Shiva Kumar
Spouse
Neubauer
Devin
1) Kary Ishwaran
2) Miah Ishwaran
1) Kaplan Tate
2) Fischer Reid

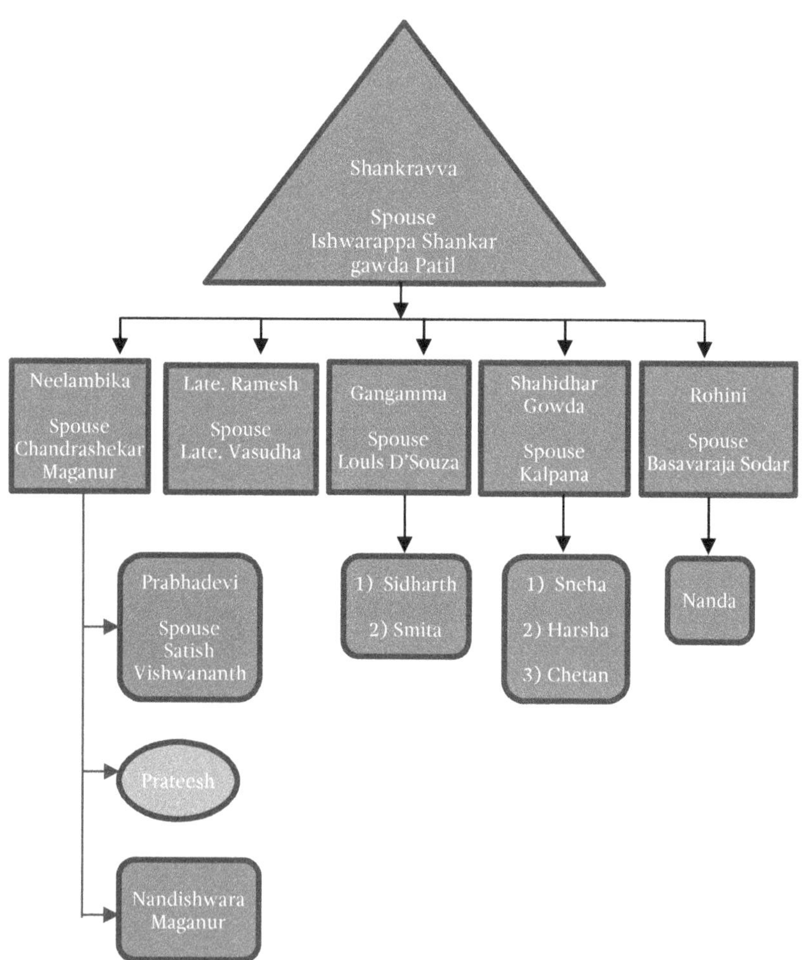
Shankravva
Spouse
Ishwarappa Shankar gawda Patil
Neelambika
Spouse
Chandrashekar Maganur
Late. Ramesh
Spouse
Late. Vasudha
Gangamma
Spouse
Louls D'Souza
Shahidhar Gowda
Spouse
Kalpana
Rohini
Spouse
Basavaraja Sodar
Prabhadevi
Spouse
Satish Vishwananth
1) Sidharth
2) Smita
1) Sneha
2) Harsha
3) Chetan
Nanda
Prateesh
Nandishwara Maganur

CHAPTER ONE

The birth of a child

In this world, somewhere on a world map you can find India a large country; look for Karnataka, one of the states, in middle South with the Capital Bangaloru. And find Dharwad, a university town. Near Dharwad and Hubli, a small point on the map shows a small village named Hiremallur.

A tiny agriculture village of about 700 families Hiremallur was not a poor village; it was surrounded by rich black soil, growing a variety of produce: wheat, cotton, and peanuts.

On this day in November 1922, a young mother named Basawa had returned with her fist born son to Hiremallur. She had gone home to Bettadur for the birth, as was the custom in those days, so her mother and sisters could care for her the first few weeks.

A priest was called to baptise the baby and also an astrologer would be consulted to predict the baby's future. They gave the boy the name of:

Ishwaran Gouda Patil. Ishwaran meaning, God and Gouda meaning farmer, Patil being his father's name, belonged to the farmer's caste system.

The astrologer checked his many charts, mumbled some mantras and announced most surprisingly that this baby boy would study much, work hard and go abroad for more studies and meet the Queen of England, Queen Mary and King George.

How would the life of this little boy develop? Would he be a teacher like his father or go away to experience new worlds? Would he grow up and become a farmer, cultivate the land; grow golden wheat fields to feed many people in his village?

Was it written in the stars; the gods had decided, or was it just Destiney?

The day this child was born was a special day for Chennappa and Basawa Patil in Hiremallur.

The young couple lived with a joint family under one roof.

The new born baby had a lot of relatives to care for him, to rock the cradle to put him to sleep after his coconut-oil bath, to pick him up when he woke up and cried, to give the baby his mother to breast feed him. All loved him, the boy with his easy smile and dimpled cheeks.

When Chennappa became the village primary school teacher, he was allowed to build his own house, a home for a single family.

Homes in Hiremallur were built up of clay and beams of wood.

An open veranda in front would lead through an entrance to a hall divided between a stable on one side and the living area on the other side, a raised gallery was where the family would sit, sew, chat and care for the little ones. Through an entrance we find the kitchen and open fire - place, the grinding stone and cooking equipment. Another door led to the sleeping area, with a large mosquito net folded up and hung up, sleeping mats and mattresses also rolled up were neatly stashed in the corner.

In the evening after a hard day's work the men of the family and some other visiting farmers would sit on the front porch to relax, smoke and chat, while waiting for dinner to be ready and served by their wives.

The conversation was usually about the crops, the weather, politics and the newly established co-op. At times when the women had done their chores and ate their dinner, they would come too, to join in for more gossip and probably the latest news about Gandhi and the uprising against the British.

CHAPTER TWO

Basawa

Basawa would be the first one up in the early morning, looking after the baby, washing him, nursing him and then she carried him on her hip. She would light the open fire in the kitchen, rubbing her eyes hurting from the escaping smoke until the firewood burned fully. Then adding a few cow dung patties to the fire, the cooking could start. But milking the buffalos had to be done first. She measured the milk, kept one small pot of milk for the family and the rest in a jar for the milkman to pick up. Then she would heat water to make the tea and a large pot of water for Chennappa's morning's bath and shave.

While Chennappa was bathing she prepared a light breakfast of upama, a preparation of cream of wheat, (rawa,) with onions and herbs and chilies, with a little yogurt on the side.

Chennappa got dressed, ate his breakfast and left for the school. The school would start early with a mid-morning break so the student could go home and eat a full meal have a rest and return for the afternoon.

Basawa started cleaning and chopping the vegetables and washing the rice, the mixing jowar flour with water and some salt, to make the dough for the roti.

"Come on Pappu, it is time for your bath and morning slumber!"

She poured hot water into a container mixed with cold water and warmed some coconut -oil in a cup she got ready in the bath room corner next to the kitchen, for baby Ishwaran's morning bath and massage.

Even though the baby was screaming loudly, she lay him down on her bare legs, face up and started pouring a little bit of oil in is ears, nose and eyes. "Now oil on your curly hair, my darling boy, I rub it softly so your hair will be soft and luscious, and your Appa will be happy to see you when he comes home. Next, I will massage your little chubby arms legs and tummy, you do like that, don't you, and you have stopped crying."

Then she turned him over and rubbed and massages his back.

Now it was time to hold him in a sitting position and slowly pour warm water over his head and body. This was not too comfortable for this little fellow. He started whining a bit but soon bath time ended and after drying and wearing a clean shirt and diapers he could fill his tummy with his mother's milk. "Now my Pappu in your cradle you go, I'll rock you and you will sleep for a long time, so I can get on with my work!" She sang a little lullaby and soon the baby was fast asleep.

Basawa could now finish cooking the dinner and make the roti.

"I'll make okra curry today, "she thought to herself aloud: They had a lovely harvest of the wonderful vegetable enough to take some to the market and exchange for grains to grind into flour and make the daily roti.

She boiled the milk, skimmed off the cream to make butter and a part of the warm milk was made into fresh yogurt so they had fresh yogurt with the dinner every day.

The buffalo's and the oxen were collected by herders; father and son, who would go to several homes to collect the cattle and herd them all to the fields outside the village in the grasslands where they could graze until evening, and be brought back to the stables of the homes.

A small boy of a year of twelve came to help Basawa by bringing in fire wood, clean the stable, sweep the veranda and front of the house all for a few pennies a day! The boy's name was Sanjay; His family had been with Chennappa's family for many years. At times Sanjay would carry the baby around the home and stable or outside when the temperature was comfortable for the little one.

"Good morning Amara, are you alright? What can I do first for you?"

"Oh, good morning Tamma, I am fine. Could you go to the well to bring some drinking water? The water vessels are empty this morning after the bath. I have just enough coals left to boil the drinking water."

Chennappa came home, after washing his face, hands and feet, he heard the baby crying and picked him up out of the cradle, "Heh you, my maga, why are you crying? Just hungry I guess, your mamma is making the roti for me, she is busy, and you just have to wait a little longer for your milk. But I can change your nappies for you, alright?" said the father. The baby started to giggle and wiggle in Chennappa's arms already feeling better after the change of diapers. Basawa finished preparing the dinner. She settled the baby on her hip and served the food to Chennappa who sat down on a wooden board on the kitchen floor. "Today's food is very tasty Basu; did you have a special ingredient?" He asked his wife. "Yes, I was able to get fresh okra and at the market exchanged it with my butter for grains to make flour. The buffalo that just had her calf gave creamier milk so I could make butter today," she answered gleefully.

In India it is tradition that the wife serves first the children, then her husband and guests, only the men. Then when everyone is satisfied and relaxed with a smoke or chewing a pawn, the women gather in the kitchen and amongst a lot of chatting and laughing and then will be able to eat themselves.

The pots and pans get cleaned the next morning, by a maid if the family can afford it otherwise the woman has to add that to the many chores she has to do during the day.

Bassawa grew up in a joint family where women helped each other, and the Matriarch usually did only the cooking and some care of the babies. Bathing the newborn was always the grandmother's task, which she loved doing. Now in her own single home, Basawa had a lot more chores.

Basawa was a very pretty young woman, sturdy build but slim, with very elegant capable hands. Her long black hair was always done up in a long braid down her back. She had dimpled cheeks when she smiled.

She preferred to wear the traditional red and orange sari of Karnataka, with a yellow or red tight, short cotton blouse. Most likely there was a tailor in the village who sewed all the women and children's clothes.

She wore small gold earrings and a nose bud and four gold bangles, which were given to her on her marriage. A black tattooed dot in the middle of her forehead that too was tradition, only for married women.

Her small hands were really strong though, she could grind the grains turning the large grinding stones and shake the flour clean from the hulls with a flat basket weaved tray made especially for this purpose.

She preferred doing this outside so the hulls would fly away in the wind.

And she could meet friends to greet and gossip with!

Basawa had no schooling; she couldn't even sign her own name!

She would use a thumbprint whenever her signature was required which was seldom. Chennappa took care of all the formalities.

Chennappa tried to teach her when they got married, but Basawa always said," I do not need to read and write, I can add and calculate the cost of every item on the market! That is all I need to know!

The Patil family in Hiremallur belonged to the Lingayat community and the Lingayat religion.

They were strict vegetarians. No eggs, fish, or meat. The food was mainly legumes, grains and coconuts, all kind of nuts, vegetables and dairy products. The water- buffaloes gave most of the milk, some people had one cow, and some villagers had goats for milk and meat.

The cow is the holy animal in India, and Hindu families cannot eat beef.

Lingayats do not have a temple of their own; they go to Hindu or Brahman temples on special occasions like weddings, or festivals.

All Lingayat families have a small prayer corner or alcove in the home where a portrait of their religious leader Basavanna, is displayed. Devotees pray at home, put with fresh flowers; light incense sticks and rub a stone made of holy ashes. Some families have images of other Hindu gods too in their puja room. Especially the gods who protect women and children and the ones promoting education, like Ganesh!

Basawa was a true believer and taught her children too how to pray and meditate before the gods every day after the bath.

Chennappa too did not skip one day of prayer before going out in the morning to work; to the school or work on to the fields.

Chennappa always wore white clothes, loose white pants, a white long shirt and a white turban.

His clothes had to get washed daily and dried in the sun to bleach them.

Basawa would take the laundry to the river bank to wash them, and most likely took a bath there too, some women bathed in the river and sometimes at home, especially during the rainy season!

CHAPTER THREE

Diwali Festival

Baby Ishwaran, was only a few weeks old when it was Diwali the celebration of light.

"Husband, next week is Diwali and what are we going to do? Our baby is well adjusted, not crying too much and I am feeling strong and can make our Diwali dinner this year in our own home," announced Basawa. "That is a good plan, Basu, but big brother Karigoudar has invited us already, and I have accepted their invitation. Your time is still very occupied with the baby, and making a whole dinner might be too much for you. You could go over to their house and give a helping hand to your sisters -and mother in-law." "I thought it would be nice to have Ishu's first Diwali in our own home, but it might be a little too much for us, so we'll spend it with the family in the big house." Basawa reluctantly agreed.

"Big brother Karigoudar is going to town tomorrow with the oxen cart, and I can go with him to buy the necessary groceries for the feast.

Tell me what you need like; oil for our Diwali lights, sugar, white flour, and any other things we need for Diwali," said Chennappa.

"We need some new baby clothes for our son, he has been wearing all hand me downs from the family, for Diwali he needs a new shirt and panty," suggested Basawa.

Karigoudar, Chennappa's brother had his bullock cart ready to go to the town. The oxen had been hosed down the horns polished and colourful ribbons tied to them. "Brother, come, hurry up, we've got to leave now to be in town on time for the market, I have a long list of supplies to purchase," said his brother.

"And we still have to return in the evening." Chennappa came running, put his bags in the cart and climbed on the front seat next to his brother. "Off we go to town, my brother, we have a long way to go," he shouted cheerfully. It was a once in a while outing for the brothers who enjoyed it thoroughly!

They were on their way, traveling along the dusty roads, through the growing jowar fields, to the hills of the next town, which was awakening with the rising sun; it was a day of promise.

Chennappa was planning to visit the home of their cousin Patil, and meet some old school friends, do some shopping and buy a new sari for his wife, and a small embroidered shirt for his son, as was the custom at Diwali.

Everyone was happy to see him and congratulate him with the birth of his son Ishwaran.

The brothers went to the market and bought all the necessary ingredients for the feast; white sugar, jaggery, white flour, cooking oil. salt, channa dhal for the holigi and the sambar.

"Chennappa Patil, how are you?'" asked someone suddenly surprised. "Oh, Namaskara Chandra, good to see you, how are you?" The two friends greeted each other with pleasure and relayed all the latest family news instantly.

Chendru asked his friend about his marriage: "congratulations, I heard you got married?" "Yes, my wife is Basawa from Bettaduru, and we just had a son, a few weeks old, a healthy bouncing baby, we are truly blessed," answered Chennappa.

"And you have a primary school in Hiremallur, how many students do you have? We on the other hand are still waiting for our school and teacher; we have been looking for one for some time now." Chandra felt envious.

Chennappa told his friend he has 10 boys and three girls in the school, and that he is encouraging other parents to send their girls too.

"But most of the girls are busy helping mother in the kitchen and with other chores.

The girls need to learn to make the roti; it is a real task to make them right. That reminds me Chandra, I want to buy some story books for the school, can you direct me to a good book store?"

"Sure, come along I'll take you" the two set of in search of the book store, there were several small ones with local newspapers, magazines and advertisements, but Chennappa wanted a book store with stories and literature for academic studies. There were no books at all in the small school building in Hiremallur.

Footnote

The primary school system was established in 1868. The state law made That Primary education was compulsory for children between six and eleven years of age. But not all girls went to school and most of the girls would leave at age ten. During the harvest season the school is only partly open because older children need to help parents on the fields.

For further education the children had to enter the middle school in the next village. Some walked up and down, some board with friends or relatives. Only a few boys leave the village for further education.

Chennappa had to pay these out of his own pocket, maybe later he could get a refund from the school board, but he was not counting on that!

The town had a college, several high schools, a Christian English medium school and plans for a university up on the hills.

Chennappa looked up to the hill and imagined a tall tower of Karnataka University, and said to himself," I will save all my paisa's for my sons so they can to go to the University one day".

"Look, here is the book store, I will leave you here and say good bye, it was wonderful seeing you again after so many years, and I am pleased to hear all is well with you and the family, good bye friend until we meet again." Chandra said and embraced his friend, to go to his own home and start preparation for his own feast. "Namaskar, see you dear friend," said Chennappa and entered the bookstore.

Chennappa had a budget given to him by the school board. The students needed slate and slate -pencils, notebooks and pencils, all that, but it did not allow for storybooks.

Chennappa was concerned about the general knowledge of his students and had a curriculum planned to teach history and geography besides arithmetic and alphabets.

He had gone to the local potter and asked for some clay to make Diwali lamps with the children the next day back at school.

Karigoudar and Chennappa arrived back home late in the evening, they unloaded the bullock cart and entered their homes, tired but very satisfied with the day and all the purchases.

"Look here mother of my son, I brought you a new green sari and an embroidered white shirt for our son, ready to wear for Diwali."

Proudly Chennappa presented the gifts to Basawa, who was really very pleased and smiled gently at her husband.

Next day Basawa got up early after milking and cooking breakfast she started cleaning the home from top to bottom as was customary, even the floors were washed and spread over with a cow dung polish until it shined brightly!

Then she filled all the small mud lamps with coconut oil and place them around the house and on the veranda outside to lit as soon as it got dark.

In the evening, dressed in their new clothes, the family went to the big brother's home, carrying a small-lit oil lamp and put it outside on the veranda of brothers' home. The whole village was lit up with the Diwali lights; it looked beautiful and peaceful, ready to celebrate the festival of light.

Chapter Four

Disappointments

When the little boy was about one-year-old, he had learned to say many words, improving his vocabulary daily to the delight of his father who taught him new words every day. "One day, Ishu you will become a story teller or a teacher, my little son, "said Chennappa proudly.

Ishu could walk and could eat regular food and drink out of a cup.

When Basawa tried to hand feed him, he pushed her hand away, and said:" I can eat by myself now!"

Basawa informed Chennappa that she was pregnant again.

With a loud voice Chennappa called out," Oh Basu, maybe another son, it could be a farmer, it looks like the first one is going to be a scholar, he is smart and talks already! Did you hear that Ishu, you are going to get a little brother or sister!"? Said Chennappa, picking up his son and hugging him tightly.

Basawa was feeling somewhat nauseous and tired, "Husband, could you look after Ishu for a while, I need to lie down for a short nap," she requested. She went into the sleeping room pulled out a mattress and laid down for a well-deserved rest.

"Come son, you are going to stay with uncle in the big house for a few days. Your mother needs some time off to rest, she is not feeling well."

Ishwaran was a bit surprised because Awwa was never ill, she never stayed in bed, she was always up early to milk the buffalo's, light the kitchen fire, and mix the dough for the roti.

But Ishwaran was happy to go the big house, he would have fun playing with his cousins, the bigger girls would take him for a walk around the village, greet neighbours and friends.

This time the older cousins took him to the water tank in the coconut grove. It was nice and cool there. Two of the boys jumped into the water and dog paddled around the tank. "The water is so cold, brrrr," they screamed, and climbed out immediately. Ishwaran was giggling cheerfully.

He ate his dinner and went to sleep right away.

Chennappa came over to tell the women of the family, that Basawa had a miscarriage, "the midwife came and gave her some soothing tea, she is asleep at the moment, but she needs a few days to recover. Could you please keep my son for a few more days?" asked Chennappa.

He felt very sad and disappointed, and concerned for his wife's health too. But Basawa was a strong woman and she was well informed about the life and health of the village women.

"Oh sure," answered sister-in-law, "I will go over and stay with her tonight and tomorrow too if she needs me." "We are very sorry, Brother, you were looking forward to having another son, didn't you?"

"Yes, we were very happy, but we are young and strong, we'll try again in time."

In the evening, Karigoudar dropped by to inquire how Basawa was doing. Chennappa told him she was all right and sleeping soundly together with Ishu.

"I have been thinking, brother, about our trip to the town and all the news we heard about Gandhi and his Satyagraha. We here in the village seldom get the latest news. Our elders in the Panchayats decide over our future and what is best to saw and harvest during the seasons.

The controller comes regularly to collect our taxes, we pay whenever we can and we do not concern ourselves about the politics of the State and our Country!" Karigoudar looks seriously at his brother, who has made an important observation, something he had been thinking about too. "Satyagraha, Ghandi's concept of non-violent resistance against the British rule. Our congress leadership is working to achieve self-rule for our country, India. How can we participate?" He continued.

"We can wear cotton clothes made by Indian hands only, and boycott imported British goods." Said Chennappa. "Let's tell our wives, and relatives, also the elders from the Panchayat." "Yes, I agree," replied Karigoudar.

They finished smoking their cigarettes said goodnight and retired for the night, to begin early morning refreshed with new ideas.

Chapter Five

A little brother

Basawa recovered soon from the miscarriage and continued taking care of the home and family. Her sister's in-law was very kind and helpful, as according to tradition, joint families in the village would take care of their own relatives.

Chennappa gave a slate and pencil to Ishwaran, so he could draw and also start learning to write the Kannada letters of the alphabet.

It kept the little fellow busy for a while so that Basawa could get on with her chores.

Toys were mostly hand made out of wood; animals, blocks, English letters and numbers. Toddlers also played with small colourful pebbles.

And so, the days were spent, the months and the years.

Basawa had been pregnant again a few times but could not carry the child to maturity, until finally she knew and felt that this time, she would give birth to another child! Secretly she was wishing for a girl, but she knew Chennappa wanted a boy!

And it was a healthy baby boy! They named him Ninganagouda that means gift of God. Many Indian well-known politicians were named Niganagouda. Ishwaran was proud to be a big brother and did his best to be helpful to his mother, by rocking the cradle when baby was crying, handing her diapers, towels and clothes when it was baby's bath time.

While rocking the cradle Basawa and Ishu sang a lullaby about an elephant that lost its way, "Any bant o wany!"

Ishwaran became sleepy too and Basawa put him to bed too, soon both little boys were fast asleep and Basawa could finish cleaning the pots and pans, wash the baby clothes and have a bath herself.

But before her bath she had to grind the wheat into flour with her own grinding stones, a very tasking chore, which she handled expertly churning, churning, with her delicate but strong hands.

When the children woke up. Chennappa took them both outside on the veranda.

"Appa, tell us a story" asked Ishu, who knew his father was a good storyteller. Chennappa recited a few songs and told a story about the life of their Saint Basaveshwara.

Being a teacher Chennappa taught the children the alphabets in a song to make it like a memory game for the little boys.

And when they were a bit older, he would start to teach them the timetables as well.

CHAPTER SIX

The Cobra

During the 1920's, the surrounding rough grass fields were not only for the buffalos to graze, but also used as "bathroom for the inhabitants. They did not have outhouses or indoor facilities that came much later.

Ishwaran was now old enough to go by himself to the field to relieve himself.

He took a water can and called out: "Awwa, I am going to the field" and left whistling a happy tune.

He searched for a clean spot, put down his water can and just started to pull down his short pants when suddenly right in front of him a large cobra popped up, cissing at him hood blown out its tongue flicking in and out staring right in to his little face! Ishwaran stood as if hypnotized, petrified, not moving, then turned around and ran home calling: "Appa, Awwa, a cobra a big snake" His whole body was shivering feeling as if he was bitten. Basawa picked him up checked arms and legs but did not find bite marks, thank God! "Oh, maga, my son, you are not hurt, you are fine, just so scared! Come wash your face and Appa will take you out to a safer place later." While taking his son as soon as Ishu was quieted down a bit, Chennappa started telling the boy about the cobra snake and why it is a sacred animal.

The King cobra is the sacred animal of our god Shiva; it is wrapped around Shiva's neck to keep him from danger.

A cobra is just as scared of you as you are of it. They attack when it is frightened and to defend itself it blows up its hood to make it look much larger. When a cobra is hungry it goes out to hunt for small animals a mouse, a rat or a rabbit and even for small snakes. To be able to catch its prey it slides noiselessly closer to the animal, stands up and hypnotizes its prey by staring into its eyes. The animal cannot move or run away it is paralyzed by fear and the snake swallows it alive and whole, where the remains would get digested inside the snake, along its intestines.

Basawa added to the story a myth that if you put out a dish with some milk, the snake will quietly move away. "Yes, I remember Basu, once there was a very large cobra under your bean plants in your garden patch, you put out the milk and we all watched the very long snake slide away and disappear." Told Chennappa.

"King Cobras are worshipped all over the world, in practically all religions, you know my son, one can find several legends in multiple languages too." said father to his son.

Naga Panchami celebration

A snake idol made of clay will look at bit like this one.

When Basawa awoke she remembered that this day would be celebrating Naga Panchami, de festival of worshiping the cobra, the sacred snake of God Shiva.

Special dishes would be prepared and the Puja room cleaned and readied for the worship of Naga.

The children would wear new clothes and the young women of the village were going to put up a large swing on the largest tree in the middle of the village and all take turns to swing and sing and have fun.

The special sweet dish is Kadabu. Some were deep-fried and some steamed. A kadabu is a dumpling filled with coconut, jaggery sugar and channa dhal. All mixed and grind together. The dumpling is made of white flour dough.

Basawa could make these excellently. Her mother had taught her how to make these and also holigi.

Kadebu can be crispy deep-fried or steamed. Basawa made both. Papadams and sticky rice would complete the festive food celebrations.

Sanjay, the servant boy came and brought a soft fresh lump of clay to make a snake idol for the puja. Ningana started jumping up and down, clapping in his hands and shouting out: "Now we can make a snake, our Naga idol."

He started right away with a little help from his brother they produced a wonderful serpent.

When the food was ready, Basawa had to bathe first before she could perform the puja.

She cleaned and polished al the implements in the prayer room, lit the arthi and some incense sticks, then she poured a little milk over the idol offered some of thc food on a silver tali, recited the devotional song and meditated on her Shivalinga. The two little boys watched their mother and made also the namaskara to the Idol.

Then the family sat down for the delicious dinner.

CHAPTER SEVEN

First day at school

Chennappa called the boys and told them, "Ishu and Ningu you are now old enough to go to school.

Ishu, after breakfast take your brother and come to the school, bring your slates and pencils."

Ishwaran felt very grown up and responsible, a feeling he kept for the rest of his life.

He took his brothers' hand and they walked together to their very first school day.

They were the youngest students in the class, and were welcomed with a cheer!

The children in Hiremallur had no benches; they sat on the floor on a large coconut- woven mat.

Spellbound they listened to their teacher, their Appa, who was reading from a history booklet about the life if they're religious leader: Basaveshwara. Then they practiced and learning to write the letters of the Kannada alphabet. They would learn to write and read and were on their way to the wide world of knowledge!

Basawa asked the boys how their first day at school was, and she was delighted to hear their bright happy voices telling her about everything they did and what they learned. After a wash and a snack, they went outside to play with friends and their cousins.

Some of the games they played were: Hide and seek when young and old could participate. Other games for older boys were: gilly dandu, a game with two sticks one short and one longer one. A game similar to base -ball or cricket, also "marbles" but with small pebbles.

The girls would usually play jacks, also with small colourful pebbles.

One day coming home after school Susana, the midwife, met them at the entrance telling them their mother had given birth to one more baby another boy. Mother and son were doing fine and both were asleep, "do not make any noise boys, your mom needs rest," she told them.

The little baby was named Shiva Kumar, meaning: Son of God.

He grew up to be a beautiful, very intelligent child, loved by all in the large family. When he was five years old, he too went to school with his brothers and turned out to be one of the best students Chennappa ever taught.

One more child was born a few years later, a girl named Shankrawa.

She brought a lot of joy to the family. Ishwaran always kept a special place in his heart for his sister.

CHAPTER EIGHT

Going to the Fair

One morning Chennappa came running home from the fields with great news: "Pack up food, bedding and clothes, we are going to the fair in Sirigere, he shouted ". The High Priest of the Sirigere Matt is holding a special fair for the coming Basava Jainty festival." We are all going, Big brother and his family, little brother, Nelama and children are coming too" Basawa had never been to a fair! "Do we have to walk a long way?" she asked, I have to carry this little baby girl of ours!" "Worrywart, we are going with the bullock cart. I am making a cover for it so that your heads will not get too hot on the long journey.

We will be traveling for two days, so make sure we have enough of everything for the trip.

We will stay two days in Sirigere and then two more days to travel back" he replied.

"One servant will stay home to take care of the cattle and watch the house, while we are away."

Early the next morning the family was ready, two wagons full of noisy laughing people left the village, waving goodbye to neighbours and friends. The bullock cart was decorated with colourful ribbons, and also the two big bullocks had red ribbons tied to their long horns.

It was a happy time for everyone. At night the company found a field with some trees and bushes, where they could camp overnight. After eating their picnic food of rice with yoghurt some thick dhal and hard roties, a delicacy for the hungry crowd, the tired travelers rolled out their bedding and slept soundly on the hard, rough ground.

The happy family set off the next morning for another day of travel; they would reach Sirigere in the evening.

On reaching the town, they met many friends and relatives who greeted them happily. The bullocks watered and fed and a place for the wagon found this was where they would stay for those two days of entertainment.

A nutritious meal would be served in a large hall; every devotee was welcome and received a full meal served on a clean banana leaf. Students of the Matt and the village boarding school cooked the food for the thousands of people in the large kitchen of the Matt.

A procession was planned for the next morning, and all the people lined up along the village roads.

The boys stood and watched, mesmerized, holding tightly onto the hands of her little sister.

Elephants, acrobats, clowns and finely the high priest passed by. The priest was sitting on top of a large elephant in the shade of a small tent like umbrella. A cloth, woven with gold thread was draped over the elephant's back.

The Swamiji received garlands, fruits and money as gifts, and he blessed every one of his devotees with a smile on his holy face. A large group of priestly young students followed the Swamijie's elephants.

The boys were dressed in orange clothes and had shaved heads. One amongst them was a chubby little fellow with a kind round face. He would be the chosen one to be the future High priest of the Matt and ride through the town on his own elephant years later. And amongst of his many responsibilities would be; the destiny of young students, who needed his support to be able to further their education.

After the parade the villagers were allowed to enter the Matt and pay their respect to the other Swamijies.

Basawwana and her family went too, they climbed up to a reception room upstairs, with a balcony facing the front yard of the math. A colourful crowd was gathered in front of the gate.

Basawa had never before seen such a beautiful sight; she just stood quietly and stared at the sea of colours beneath her. Ladies in their best saris, men in mostly white clothes and white turbans and young girls with long skirts and matching tops, sparkling in the bright sunlight.

The older retired priests lived in private rooms in the Matt. Ishwaran and his brothers were too deeply moved by the holy presence of the ancient father of the monastery. They bowed down and touched their forehead to the Swamijie's feet. Their father and mother did the same and offered some fruits and money.

The holy face of the senior priest glowed with inner piece; he had a kind word for every devotee, and especially gave a loving touch to the heads of the little children.

The most amazing fun for the children was when they were allowed to feed peanuts to the elephants in the stable's downstairs.

"Well," said Chennappa," I think we should go back to our wagon, have something to eat and take an afternoon nap, we will still have a long night ahead of us."

The wagons were parked outside the village in a large field. To water them, water had to be brought from the village well or from a pump near the Matt.

While the children and grandmother had their nap, Basawa and other women of the group went to the riverbed to wash the clothes and at the same time take their baths. The clothes were draped over the rocks at the side of the river to dry; this would not take long in the hot sun, with the soft wind blowing too. This was a time of socializing for the women; laughter and happy voices could be heard for miles around.

Evening set, and now it was time to gather around the flagpole for the Indian flag raising ceremony. The Swamiji and guest speakers were already seated and facing in the direction from where the full moon would appear over the horizon. At exactly six o' clock the flag was raised and the full moon started to appear, while a few young girls sang the national anthem. The headmaster of the local school had chosen the girls for this special occasion. A band of local musicians were given the opportunity to liven up the gathering with some folk songs and a prayer. Afterwards it was time to educate the devotees.

The Chief guests were to deliver their speeches, a long-drawn-out recital of advice and praise of the Swamijie's good works improving the lives of his community.

The Swamijie's talk was about the life of the religious leader Basaveshwara and the prayers in the form of poems and songs, which preach healthy living, hard work, service to the community and devotion to God Shiva.

During the speeches, the full moon was rising over the horizon, looking like a huge yellow balloon, while in the West the sun was slowly setting, leaving an orange glow in the sky.

Shivakumar was sitting next to the grandmother, "Look Amma, the moon is so big and bright tonight." The little boy's eyes sparkled with excitement; he clapped in his hands and laughed out loud. Grandmother patted his head softly and told him he should listen to what they are trying to tell us and remember their wise words. "But Amma, those talks are too long and I can't follow them very well yet, I am still very little!" was his reply.

The loving Grandmother smiled and thought the child was right, the talks were as usual too long and somewhat boring.

Only when the High Priest was talking the crowd paid full attention, even the babies were quiet.

The sun had set, and the hills and fields were covered with silvery moonlight, a sight and moment that Ishwaran would cherish for a long time.

Later in the evening a local company would perform a drama that would last all through the night.

Usually, the play would be about the life of a famous saint of their religion. Or a play about the life of Basaveshwara. The crowd assembled in a large hall outside the Math. The hall was a temporary structure of bamboo poles covered with large coconut leaves. Long large carpets covered the earthen floor. Women and children sat together on one side and the men on the other side of the hall. Segregation was strict protocol.

Tired but happy the family packet up early next morning and left for the journey back home.

This time there was not so much singing on the way, but more of chatting and gossiping. They had heard a lot of news about relatives and friends. They all were eager to tell these stories to the rest of the family back home.

CHAPTER NINE

Troubled times

It was evening time and a cool wind played with little Shankrawa's loose hanging long black hair. It had been the day for her hair to get bathed, massaged with coconut oil and rinsed with lots of nice hot water. The Grandmother usually did this for the children in the family when the mothers were too busy with the household chores. It had been very hot and dry for many long days. The evening was a bit cooler and it would have been a nice evening were it not for the worried looks and somber voices the young girl observed while walking through the village. Coming to her uncle's house she went inside to try to find out from the women what the trouble was. She stood in a corner listening to the gossip for a while until one of the aunts discovered her and invited her to come and sit with them on their veranda. 'What brings you here with such a worried expression on your sweet face, Tangy?" asked her aunt.

The little girl was shy, and with a soft voice replied," What is the matter Auntie, everyone is looking so sad has a bad thing happened?" "No, my dear girl, not yet, but the rains have not come yet, and the fields are dry, the new seedlings are dying. It will be a bad time for many farmers if we don't get rain soon." answered her aunt. "Are the wells going to dry up too?" Shankrawa had heard stories about a terrible drought told by her grandmother. When the well was almost dry, people had to walk many miles to be able to collect a bit of muddy water from a cattle pond. Many villagers, especially the children got sick with typhoid, many also died. The cattle had roamed on dried up fields and were skin and bones. Often the cows had no milk to give. Resulting in hunger and thirst for all with many diseases developing.

But then the water tank under the coconut trees had been built and now provided clean drinking water for the villagers.

Her Aunt tried to reassure her," We are praying that this will not happen this year, Tangy, don't you worry, you be a good girl and give alms to the poor, say your prayers daily and God will make the rains come soon." I will say an extra prayer to our patron goddess. Auntie" said the serious looking girl.

But the rains did not come; all the prayers could not change the weather conditions. It was getting hotter and dryer. All the little plants in the fields died, it became a dry dusty place, and the wind blew dust into the village homes and making life even more miserable than it already was.

The water level of the river receded day by day, also the bucket to draw up water from the well had to go down deeper and deeper to reach the drinking water. The people would come together and sit idle on their front steps and grumble, quarrel, shouting at each other and blame the village drunk or the gambler for the wrath of the gods bestowed upon their land. The women had to ration the food; only the children would get a little milk in their weak tea. And only the workingmen would get a bit of sour milk with the food. The women had to do without and eat what was left over after the men and children ate. The cows and the buffaloes gave less and less milk because there was no grass to graze on the fields and only drops of water left in the cattle pond. At night the cattle were restlessly lowing and moving around in the stables. And the exhausted family members had to go to bed hungry. They too had sleepless nights. It was a very bad time, and hopefully this year the rain would come soon.

Chennappa and his older brother Karigoudar decided to call the village Panchayat together to discuss the serious situation.

The Panchayat was made up of five senior members, who were chosen by the villagers to make any decisions and oversee disturbances and unlawful behaviour.

At the meeting, called by Karigoudar and Chennappa it was suggested that the two brothers would go to the city and meet with the municipality members to get advice and help with managing the draught. So it was decided and the brothers would leave the next day early morning. They wrote down a request and all five members of the Panchayat signed it.

Karigoudar and Chennappa took the bullock cart to town and went to the Municipal offices to request for a hearing. They received an appointment for the next morning and stayed the night with relatives. Next morning the Panchayat Rai was ready to receive them and hear their stories. Heremallur was not the only village in trouble during the draught. The municipal members heard them complain and after a short intermission came back with the report:

The corporate members would reduce the agriculture income tax.

And we recommended every village to build a reserve water tank, to be able to collect more rainwater during the rainy season to be prepared next year if the rains are late or not sufficient to irrigate the fields.

It was a very hot day, Ishwaran and his brother Ningu were sitting on the front steps of their home, wiping their faces with a small towel.

"Oh, it is so hot today, my head aches, I am sweating, I don't feel like eating anything, only drinking cold water," growled Ningu.

"Yes, brother I feel the same, what to do?"

"I have an idea, let's go swimming," suggested Ishwaran.

Ningu always ready for an adventure with his brother asked, "where?" "You know, the water tank where the coconut trees grow?" told Ishwaran.

"You can swim there?" Ningu was really surprised to hear that.

"Yes, I went once with our cousins, they showed me how to swim, just paddle fast with your arms like a dog swims and you will stay afloat. It was great," remembered Ishwaran.

"Ningu, let's go quietly, Kumar and Shankrawa are too small, and they can't come". They called cousin Viya who felt like a swim too, and off they went.

Viya and Siddu, joined them gladly to go and have a cool dip in the clear water of the tank. I was so cool and comfortable under the coconut palms. They stripped to their under wears and jumped in the water, splashing, dipping, flipping and dog-paddling.

Even Ningu who had never been in the water entered suddenly, crying out, "I do not know how to swim, I am drowning!" Moving his arms round and round losing control and was about to start sinking when Viya jumped in and pulled him out! Viya was a good swimmer he had been in the tank a lot of times. Ningu dripping wet started to laugh, "I am all wet, but really cooled off. I think I will put just my feet in the water!" It was fun.

But when they came home, Basawa greeted them with a very angry voice, "where have you been?" she asked.

"Awwa, it was so hot so we just went for a swim in the water tank" answered Ishu innocently. Basawa did not want to say anything, only," wait until your father gets home! Go and get dried up and change your clothes."

Chennappa did not get angry frequently, but when he heard that the boys went for a swim in the water tank, the water everyone needed so desperately he was furious and also disappointed in his older son! He should have known better. He called Ningu and Ishu with a loud voice, "your mother tells me that you went swimming, is that true?"

"We did, it was so hot, it seemed like a good idea to cool off," they answered back.

Chennappa shouted at them, "you two have been very irresponsible, I am very angry and disappointed in you Ishu, you should have known better, maga, you are an older brother and I need to depend on you to keep you brothers and sister safe!

Your brother could have drowned, he has never been in the river or the tank, and he never learned to swim. And secondly, we need every drop of clean water, during this draught.

Didn't you realize that you made the water dirty? We can't use it now, unless we boil the drinking –water," asked the very angry father.

"The buffalos need it, you two go now and bring two buckets of water for the cattle. And then for every home a bucket too, and tell them to boil the water when they want to drink it"

Ningu grumbled, huffing and puffing," Anna, brother, you and your bright ideas! Swimming was fun but we should have thought about keeping the water clean for our neighbours during this bad dry season"!

The boys were very sorry and kept bringing water to all the homes daily, until the rains finally came and everyone gave a sigh of relief.

CHAPTER TEN

Ganapati Celebrations

"Amma, Amma," Shankrawa; walking into the family home across the road, was calling her grandmother.

"Tomorrow is Ganapati festival, my Awwa started preparing for the celebration, Amma, are you going to make holigi too?" asked a very excited little girl. She remembered from last years the delicious food, the songs and rituals of worshipping the Ganapati idol they made of clay.

"Appa is bringing some clay from the potter's shop for his students to make a statue to take home for their own puja and some for us too, Anna and Ningu will make out Ganepati."

The grandmother arrived carrying in her hand a small rock carving of Ganapati. This little idol was a favorite of the older woman, which reminded her of many treasured memories.

"Look Tangy, I've had this small Ganesha for many years, and every year we place it again in our puja room to worship for ten days during the holidays. Look at it and observe that lord Ganapati, or Ganesh, has a human body and an elephant head" Said Grandmother and continued, "we perform the puja twice a day, once in the morning and once in the in the evening."

Ishu, Ningu and Kumar, came in looking for their sister and sat down near Amma, to listen to her story.

"Once, a long time ago, many years ago, when I was still young and had just married your grandpa, we were on our way home after a long day of hard work in the fields; I used to help your grandfather at harvest time, when suddenly I saw hiding in the long grass, a small carving of a Ganesh.

I was so delighted to find it just a day before Ganapati; the celebration of the birth of the Elephant God. This small statue has brought me a lot of good luck; I had a good husband and a loving mother in-law too!

Ganesha is the son of Parvati and lord Shiva, and as you notice he has a human body and an elephant head. He likes sweets that shows in his big tummy," continues Grandma.

"He is the Patron of: education, writing, travelling, commerce, and of starting new projects.

I will teach you a little song to sing especially when after ten days of worship all of you, with your Appa, will take the clay Idol to the river to immerse it in the water singing this song:

Ganapati, Ganapati Moray,

Pareshan karein mujhe choriyan.

But---

We always sang it like this:

Ganapati, Ganapati Moryay

Pundi palee soray!

I do not think that was right, but we as children sang it like that." she said.

The three children went home singing the small lyric.

For ten days the school children had holidays, banks and shops would be closed too for a few days.

The food was delicious, the holige mouthwatering, and reminding everyone that Ganapati loved sweets, and it shows in his big belly!

CHAPTER ELEVEN

The new school

Ishwaran was now studying in grade five and to continue his schooling he had to join the secondary school in the next town, a village really, near Hiremallur. He would be able to walk most days or get a ride with a neighbour in their bullock cart.

He had to leave home very early in the morning and come home late in the afternoon. He loved school and went with enthusiasm and studied really very hard to attain a scholarship for college education, which was his set goal! He was good in language, history and geography but math and sports were not his favorite subjects!

Some of his schoolmates who would walk together with him asked, "Why do you carry such a long stick every day to school?"

"I do, because I might see a large cobra snake hiding in the long grass, I swish my stick around to scare it away. I was surprised by a huge cobra once, never forgot the scary shock I experienced."

And that is what he did, swish, swash, swinging the stick here and there around, through the tall grassy fields.

With all this walking, Ishu's chapels were all worn out, one of the soles came lose, and he could not use it anymore.

"Appa, "he told his father," I am now in secondary school and I have to walk a lot, my chapels are all worn out, don't you think I should have a new pair of shoes?" Putting it that way, Chennappa agreed to buy a new pair of chapels for his son.

They went to the village shoe shop and bought a shiny, lovely, good fitting pair of chapels, the best in the shop!

How proud he was the next day to show his friends his new chapels.

His old worn-out pair went on the village garbage heap, good riddance!

Early one morning when Chennappa took the two water containers to go and get the water from the well as he did every day, Ishwaran came running, "Appa, Appa, wait, I'll come with you to help you," he thought his father might like some help and also thought he might show off his lovely new pair of chapels.

At the well Ishu was afraid that his new chapels would get wet and dirty in the muddy ground around the well. So he put them to the side on a dry patch of grass.

They filled their containers with the well water and were ready to carry them home when Ishu looked for his chapels in the dry grass, but they were not there! He looked around the well on all sides, everywhere, no new chapels anywhere! He cried out loudly: "I have put them right here, has anybody seen them?" Nobody had seen them; somebody must have taken them! The new chapels were gone, never to return!

He cried bitter tears at home, looking for another old pair, something that would fit him; his other pair was gone with the garbage.

"Now I have to walk on my bare feet to school," he sobbed.

His brother Kumar came from the bedroom carrying a pair of chapels that belonged to him but was still a bit too large for his small feet.

"Here Anna, you can have these, they are too big for me you can use them for school, only until you can get new ones!" His brother exclaimed.

"You are very generous my little son," said Basawa, hugging him.

"You are my best brother, Tamma, said Ishu, also giving him a hug.

So walking to school wearing his brother's chapels and working hard, Ishwaran graduated with high marks and received a scholarship for the pre- University College in Dharwar.

Chapter Twelve

Shivakumar

Ishwaran's youngest brother Shivakumar, just Kumar called at home, was a very special boy; he was smart, attentive, with a kind disposition, always ready to give a helping hand when needed.

He finished the grade five curriculum in the village school at an early age and told his father: "Appa, I am not learning anything here at your school anymore, could I go to the next school for my secondary education? I can walk together with cousin Viya, who is going too, every day." Chennappa had noticed too that this son of his was very smart and needed continuing education too, his other son, Ningu, was more of a farmer's boy and was already very useful working in the fields. So Chennappa scraped together some of his loose change and enrolled his second son into the neighbouring secondary school.

Early, very early, Kumar got up in the morning, had his bath, and got dressed in his cleanest shirt and short pants. He was ready to leave when Basawa called him back to give him something to eat and a glass of fresh milk. Usually, the boys would take a small packed lunch with them, but

Basawa had no time to get it ready for Kumar, who was so anxious to leave early on the first day of his new school. She knew and expected that the cousins might share some lunch with Kumar today, next day she would pack extra so the boys could share again.

Kumar was a good student and he enjoyed all the new subjects eagerly, he seemed to be advancing rapidly, especially in the math and science subjects. Chennappa and Basawa were very proud parents to have two sons in the continuing education programs.

Ishwaran was now studying at the Karnataka College in Dharwar and residing at the free boarding facilities at the Dharwar Lingayat Matt.

His room was like a hole in the wall, with a bed, a small table and hooks on the wall to hang his clothes. The Head Swamiji of the Matt provided free board and food, one meal a day, mostly to students from villages. That was just enough for the boys to survive and study at the schools and colleges of the town.

Ishwaran's scholarship provided him with tuition to study literature and languages; he took English, Kannada-literature and the classic language Sanskrit.

He met other students from neighbouring villages and acquired a nice circle of friends. Becoming interested in the classical literature of the Kannada and Sanskrit languages, made him think of starting to write himself and he started writing short stories and small novels in Kannada language.

Exam time was coming up; the boys would study until late at night with restless sleep. Ishwaran was tossing and turning on his narrow cot when he suddenly thought about his brother Kumar, who was sitting for his exams too! "How would he do the first year, probably quite well," he mumbled to himself. Indeed, Shivakumar passed with flying colors and would surely get a scholarship too.

Suddenly one early morning he was roused by someone calling his name: Ishu, Anna, wake up, there is a message for you, His Holiness the Swamiji wants you to come to his room immediately."

Ishwaran got dressed and ran to the Swami's living quarters and the private bedroom, knocked on the door and entered "Oh, son, Maga, there is an urgent message for you to go home right away, your brother Kumar is very sick. There are some visitors here who will leave with their bullock cart and can give you a ride half way to Heremallur, get your things ready quickly, and come to the front to meet them."

Nervously he packed up his papers, books and dirty clothes in a large canvas bag and ran to the front door of the Matt.

The bullock cart was ready and they left right away.

Ishwaran sat next to the driver and told him that he had to go home because his brother was very sick. "You live in Heremallur" asked the driver, "I know some farmers who live there too, the family Chandragoudar, do you know them?" "Oh yes very well they are good friends of my father and their fields are close to ours." My family name is Patil my father's name is Chennappa Gouda he is the primary school teacher." "Yes, I know who he is, I think I can drop you off close to your village, although you will have to walk a bit down the dusty road, about 15-20 minutes." "I do appreciate that; I am very anxious to get home as soon as possible."

Sweating and out of breath he stumbled into the home.

Calling loudly: Appa, Amma, I am home, what is wrong with my brother?"

"Shh, quiet, he is asleep. He has a lot of pain in his leg," warned Basawa.

"Go wash up and come sit down outside, I will tell you what happened," said Chennappa.

Chennappa and his son, Ishwaran were sitting outside on the front veranda while Chennappa told Ishwaran about the accident Kumar had a few days ago.

"On the walk to school a sharp stone fell on his foot, and left a small but deep cut. Kumar wiped off the blood with a piece of cloth, one of his friends used to wipe his nose, gave him, around his foot, and walked on to the school through dirt and dust. Finished the day and walked home again.

At home he washed his hands and feet, but did not clean the small wound on his foot very well. He did not tell his mother but expected the scratch to heal itself.

"Several days went by, the wound did not heal, it turned red and was painful but the boy still limped every day to and back to school.

Finally, the teacher noticed there was something wrong with Kumar, he felt feverish and moaned keeping his leg up on the bench.

He asked Kumar to take off the bandage and noticed the wound had become infected the foot and leg starting to swell up.

He gave the boy some quinine, and the only available Ayurveda medication and organized someone to take him home.

At home, right away, Basawa cleaned the wound with iodine, and let the foot soak in warm water with salt, put a clean bandage and gave Kumar a few herbs to help him sleep.

But the infection got worse, the leg swelled up and Kumar cried out with pain. And that is when we called you to come home," told Chennappa.

Ishwaran sat at his brother's bed day and nights caring for him with cold cloths, giving soothing herbal drinks and reading encouraging words from Chennappa's prayer booklets.

Nothing helped the infection increased; the leg got red and swollen, the boy crying, until he became half unconscious.

Blood poisoning got into the blood circulation; it reached his lungs and finally his heart. The boy died quietly, unconscious, in his sleep.

Ishwaran was inconsolable with the tragic loss of his younger brother. A brother who was so gifted, so gentle and intelligent, a really special child.

He was desperate to understand the loss, "why, what could we have done to prevent and cure the blood poisoning?" he thought.

Angry moods filled Ishwaran's mind, he went for a walk kicking at stones and dust wondering what they could have done to save the life of such a healthy, wonderful boy! He did not feel like going back to Dharwar and finish his exams he stayed home moody and moping. Little Shankrawa who adored her older brother and seeing him so upset and grief stricken tried to comfort him by sitting down next to him on the front steps and stroking his hands. That put a tiny smile on Ishwaran's face and he dried his tears.

Modern medicine had not reached the villages yet; they mainly cured themselves and used Ayurveda treatments, which did work at times, but not enough to stop the infection.

Family and neighbours gathered in the home to support the deeply sorrowful parents. Basawa while crying, wiping her tears started to make tea for everyone. Her sister's in-law and some of the children helped to serve the friends with hot sweet, soothing tea.

Footnote: In those days there were no anti- tetanus vaccines, no penicillin. But they did have iodine, which could have been used to clean the wound right away.

Chapter Thirteen

Coming home

Walking alongside the riverbank on his way home, young Ishwaran reflected on the past year. After his brother's death he had lost all desire to go back to college and sit for the exams. He stayed home, being lazy, just hanging around the house and helping his father on the fields once in a while. He failed the academic year, but then started to miss the college and his friends, finally returned to class and successfully graduated the next year. Now he had good news to tell his family. He had been accepted for graduate studies at the University of Bombay.

He had added to his study funds by tutoring some college students and also receiving another scholarship. Chennappa had written to him, telling him that the harvest that year was very promising and he would be able to give him some money toward his study funds.

The first person to greet him on entering the home was his little sister Shankrawa. She threw her arms around him and said:

Oh, my big brother, I am so happy that you are home" and she gave him a loud kiss. Basawa smiled at him." My son welcome home "she said and started to light the fire for tea and a nutritious snack of rava upama.

After a wash Ishwaran sat down with his family and started telling all about his studies, his friends and the latest news about Mahatma Gandhi. Basawa noticed that he was wearing a homespun cotton shirt and pants and a Gandhi cap.

"I brought the latest news paper for you Appa, with a lot about the politics and activities of our freedom fighter Mahatma Gandhi.

He is busy organizing peasants, farming communities and urban labourers to protest against excessive land taxes and discrimination. He became a leader of the National Congress, promoting many campaigns for a variety of social causes. He wears a cotton dhoti, hand woven and shawl, is vegetarian just like us, and promotes nonviolent protests.

He wants freedom and self-rule for all of India with religious pluralism, no discrimination!

You can read about a lot of his actions in the newspaper I brought, Appa. He wears a cotton dhoti, hand woven and shawl, is vegetarian just like us Lingayats. He fasted as a means of protest and self-purification.

He wants freedom and self-rule for all of India with religious pluralism, no discrimination!

You can read about a lot of his actions in the newspaper I brought, Appa. He was born on October 2nd 1869 in Porbandar, Gujarat India."

Appa, Awwa, after I finish my doctorate certificate from the Poona University, I will be teaching at the Sholarpur College in Northern Karnataka for a few years and save to go abroad and study at the Oxford University in England. That is my future plan. But I promise that I will return home when I have my degree, and then maybe get married. You here at home may be looking for a suitable wife for me after a few years, not too soon!" he exclaimed!

Full of thoughts for his future he explained his plans to the parents. They listened, hoped and also prayed that his son would be successful in achieving his goals.

Epilogue

Quote:" there is truth in History but what remains are the memories of the stories told"

The story I wrote is about a young boy growing up in a village in India.

The story is following the young boy's early years and his family coping with hardships, sickness, surviving the British rule and hard work.

My husband grew up in this village and through studies, scholarships and the benevolent gift from his family High priest was able to go to England and study for a PhD at Oxford University.

I have visited his village and observed the daily routines of the family members.

But except for personal told stories, my writing is mostly based on fiction. With the exception of the family, other people in the story are fictitious.

Enjoy the story of a special child who grew up in simple surroundings, set his goals and worked hard toward reaching them.

AFTERWORD

The real story
Accomplishments

K. Ishwaran achieved many if not all, of his goals.

During his student years Ishwaran officially changed his name from: Ishwaran Gouda Patil to: Karigoudar Ishwaran, which became: K. Ishwaran. His pseudonym in Karnataka literature became: Hiremallur Ishwaran. My married last is Ishwaran and my children last name also Ishwaran.

Ishwaran was born in a small village, Hiremallur, in Karnatak State, on November 2, 1922.

Ishwaran's father was the village schoolteacher. Being a teacher, he insisted that his children were also well educated. Ishwaran told that they would sit in the evening around an oil lamp writing their alphabets and reciting timetables.

Ishwaran's dedication to education was thus established in his childhood and carried on throughout his life. He was deeply committed to family, religion and education.

His father saved every penny to be able to send his eldest son, Ishwaran, to further his schooling in Dharwar.

While attending the High School, Ishwaran stayed as a boarder in the local Lingayat Mat. His respect for religion was instilled during those years.

He pursued his graduate studies at the University of Bombay and obtaining his first doctorate at the Karnatak University, Dharwar, in the field of ancient Indian Literature.

Thereafter he devoted seven years teaching as Principal of Sholapur College and as lecturer at Hubli College.

During these years he wrote most of his Kannada short stories and novels.

Some of these are still used as text books.

Ishwaran was also involved in the passive freedom fight, wearing only homespun cotton and a Gandhi cap.

From this literary and philosophical absorption, he turned away to widen his sphere of interest in anthropological circles at Oxford, where he worked for and obtained another research degree in the years 1954-1956. Pursuing his sociological interest further he came to the Netherlands on a research grant. He joined a two years' program at the Institute of Social Studies in The Hague and completed a Master's degree in Social Sciences. By the time he finished the degree, he had become aware of and greatly interested in the problem posed to the Sociologists by the Dutch family.

During 2 ½ years he did research; wrote the book, "Family Life in the Netherlands" and finished his doctorate from the University of Leiden, in 1959.

He made many friends in Holland; one of his friends was Wobine de Sitter, who he married later after returning to his hometown Dharwar where he accepted a position as Professor of Anthropology in 1960.

Before leaving Holland Ishwaran's managed to get a contract with Brill publications to start editing sociological journals. The International Journal of Comparative Sociology was published in 1961. And the Journal of comparative Anthropology followed soon after, sponsored by Karnatak University.

Two of their children were born in Dharwar: Arundhati born in 1962, and Hemant born in 1963.

For five years he invested all his energy in teaching, his family and friends and research of a typical Indian village, named by him Shivapur.

These studies, a trilogy, were published during 1966-1968 by Roudledge and KeganPaul, London and by Columbia University Press, New York.

At this time more research projects were still on his mind and funds were not available. Also, the University politics were very upsetting for this dynamic person. An opportunity presented itself at the right time. A visiting professorship was available in St. Johns, Newfoundland, Canada. Ishwaran applied and was appointed for a year's teaching job.

Making arrangement for his wife and children to follow him later, he joined the department of Sociology and Anthropology of Memorial University of Newfoundland, St. Johns, Canada, there he met Nels Anderson who became a very dear friend.

In 1972 Ishwaran published and edited monographs in hounor of Nels Anderson.

Even though Newfoundland has very cold winters, Ishwaran felt at home in Canada. And when a position came open for a professorship of Sociology at York University, Toronto. He decided to take it and move to Toronto.

The family immigrated to Canada in 1966, and a third child, Shivakumar was born in July 1967.

Ishwaran never stopped finding new objects of interest for his research. This time he discovered the Dutch families, immigrated to Holland Marsh, near Toronto. He received a Canada Council research grant and started his work, resulting in the book "Family, Kinship and Community". A study of Dutch Canadians. A developmental approach. Published in 1977.

Ishwaran was a dedicated teacher at York University, always concerned about the well-being of the students; many of his Ph.D. students became very close friends.

Still, he felt himself to be a rootless immigrant always missing life in India, thus every summer he went back to Dharwar to write and do more research on the Lingayat religion. He wrote his Autobiography in Dharwar in the Kannada language, although this work has not been translated into English.

Ishwaran wrote: "Religion and Society Among the Lingayats of South India" published in Kannada Language by Maysore University. Later translated by the author himself.

He completed research on the trilogy of "Monks and Monasteries" and wrote two books, "Basava and the Lingayat Religion". He was still working on the third part in Dharwar when his health failed him.

During his years at York University, he edited several textbooks: "Sociology", "Family and Marriage" and "The Canadian Family" were amongst his most extensive works.

The Journals were flourishing; by this time, he was editing four Journals:

International Journal of Comparative Sociology, the Journal of Asian and African Studies, the Journal of Developing Society and Contributions to Asian Studies.

In 1990 five Essays in Honour of K. Ishwaran; "Studies in Change and Continuity in Indian Civilization", were published and edited by Yogandra Malik and Dherandrak K. Vajpey, with contributions of renowned scholars of East Indian Society.

Retirement was not in Ishwaran future plans. He was still lecturing until his seventieth year. But now he thought it was time to start on his own and established the:" de Sitter Publishing Company" with three new Journals: "International Journal of comparative Family and Marriage", "International Journal of Comparative Religion and Philosophy" and "International Journal of Race and Ethnic Studies" They were Published in 1994-1995. Poor health and the absence of his son Shivu proved to be too much to keep the new company on an even keel; he had to give it up. Shivu was studying in England, Oxford and in Leiden, Holland. On his return to Toronto Shivu followed in his father's footsteps and launched again the de Sitter Publications.

Once Ishwaran had to fill in a questionnaire for his children's school, to the question of: what are your hobbies, he answered: reading and writing.

Anyone, whoever entered his office at York, will remember all the piles of manuscripts etc. on the floor around the room. It looked like chaos but he knew exactly where everything was!

GLOSSARY

Family names

Amma; mother or grandmother

Awwa; mother

Appa; father

Anna; older brother

Akka; older sister

Adja; grandfather

Adji; grandmother

Kakka; uncle, brother of older brother

Magalu; daughter

Maga; son

Mammy; aunt, sister of father

Tangy; younger sister

Tamma; younger brother

Soshy; daughter –in law

Pappa, pappu; baby

Community names

Basava; Leader of Lingayats who lived in the twelfth century A.D.

Basava Jayanti; birthday celebration of Basava

Chakkadi; bullock –cart

Deepavali; festival of light

Ganapati; elephant tusked god

Gilli-dandu; game with two sticks, somewhat like cricket.

Halli; village

Hiriya; elder, respectfully

Jaggery; course dark brown sugar

Jati; cast

Kadibu, sweet dish, like dumplings

Laxmi; goddess of wealth

Madi; ritual, purity

Mantra; sacred formula, incantation

Mahashivaratri; the great night of Shiva, festival

Nagarapanchami; festival of snakes

Papadam; crisp rice chip

Panchayat; village council

Purana; mythological stories

Rawa; cream of wheat

Sari; dress of Hindu women

Shiva Jayanti; birthday celebration of Shiva

Swami, priest. Maha Swamiji; High Priest

Taluka; subdivision of a district

Uru; village

Yedi; gift of food to gods

Vachana's religious songs and poems, some written by Basava, religious leader of the Lingayat religion, A.D.1300.

BIBLIOGRAPHY

Ghandi, Mohandas

Ghandi

An Autobiography, with a forward by Sissely Bok

Translated by Mahadev Desai

Beacon Press, Boston 1993

Ishwaran, K.

Foreword by Conrad Arensberg

Tradition and Economy in Village India

Routledge & Kegan Paul

London 1966

Ishwaran, K.

Religion and Society among the Lingayats of South India

Vakas Publishing House PVT LTD 1983

Ishwaran, K

Shivapur, a South Indian Village

Routledge & Kegan Paul

London,1966 By the Late VINCENT A. SMITH, CIE

THIRD EDITION edited by PERCIVAL SPEARS

THE Oxford History of India

Oxford at the Clarendon Press

Wobine Ishwaran,2007 Entrance to the Matt

Wobine Ishwaran

Sirigere Matt, 2007

Ishwaran with his mother, Basawa Patil

Basawa Patil

Basawa Patil, my mother-in law, 1987

EXPLANATION

Sirigere village and Sirigere Matt, Chitradourg. Karnataka State, India.

The Sirigere Math is the main establishment in the Sirigere village. The senior Swamiji manages the Matt, the village and all the citizens. At that time there were about 500 families living there. There was one primary school and one orphanage. The village is surround by agricultural fields and coconut trees.

All providing local crops, food and jobs for the village population. There is a large tank collecting rainwater during rainy season and irrigation is regulated during the dry season.

The main religion is Lingayat, as the Swamiji of Sirigere is a Lingayat. The religion was established in 1300 by the Guru Basaveshwara. All festivals, weddings and town meetings are presided over by the Maha Swamiji, the Head Swamiji.

The Matt and village are a community on its own.

CPSIA information can be obtained
at www.ICGtesting.com
Printed in the USA
BVHW081829170323
660662BV00003B/537